G●LDEN

wilder
∴

also by Wilder

Nocturnal
Wild Is She

Andrews McMeel
PUBLISHING®

GOLDEN

this is a trip around the sun.

a new beginning.
a celebration.
a homecoming.

you've always known
how to grow towards the light.

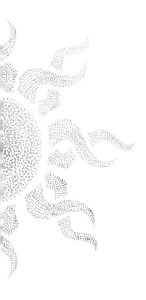

now open your eyes, the best is yet to come.

for my family,
who gives me so much
room to grow

for jess,
my sun in the middle of a
cloudy day

MAGIC HOUR

do you believe in

MAGIC

today there are no words
for the colour wild—

honest things don't need a name.

i love the way my pillow
holds on to morning.

slivers of brilliance and
shadows stain my walls
and i'm reminded that
moments of darkness were
once covered in light, too.

i blink in both directions,
to sleep and to wake,
and i smile knowing that
the colour of the sky
will always find me
even if nothing else does.

my arms are reaching out like sunrise.
it's a new day
with a sky full of promise.

a slow ascent.

and now i remember why
nothing beautiful happens quickly.

growing always takes time—

like seasons.
like change.

if today is a bad day,
i want you to know that it's okay to
pull the sheets over your head
and bury your face inside of them.
maybe screaming at the top
of your lungs into the pillows
will be your greatest act of letting go,
or maybe it will leave you with
eyes that burn and a headache that
wants to hang on for dear life,
but at least you will know
that what you're feeling is honest.

as the day moves on,
just remember that it's not
leaving without you.

it is steady.
it is constant.
it is ready when you are.

time is forever on your side
and it will never ask you to hurry.
it will never ask you to change.

that's the thing about love

sometimes it arrives when you least expect it.
it is that knock at your door on a sunday
morning. your hair is a mess and maybe
everything else is, too, but you answer
anyway because you have nothing to hide.
you find the words *thinking of you* written on a
folded piece of paper next to a handful of
wildflowers, because he remembered that
they are your favorite and wanted you to have
them, *just because*.

and sometimes it leaves when you are not
ready. it is that goodbye after you've already
fallen in love. your eyes feel like spring, but
everything around you is colder now. the
record skips at your favorite part and his
sweater doesn't fit like it used to. there are
so many questions living here, but no one to
answer them.

just remember that your heart
does not live in someone else's hands,
because the things that are meant to stay
will never leave you.

sometimes, it only takes two fingers in the air
to find your peace.

i have been following my dreams
since the day i opened my eyes.
and when they ask me how i've survived
so long with a smile on my face,
i point to the sky and remind them
that the sun rises for everyone;

no matter the season.
no matter the day.

they used to tell me
to get my head out of the clouds,
but the view up here
is too beautiful to miss.

i'm the kind of person who gives every sunrise a name. i speak in colour and listen with both arms open, ready to catch anything that may fall. i believe in magic and everything else that seems impossible because i've been collecting wishes on candles for years and i know that one day they will find their way back to me.

sometimes words hurt,
but the beautiful thing is that
they can also heal.
so don't tear the pages
out of your story that you want to forget.
instead, fold them at their corners
so you can look back and remember
how far you have come.

i'm standing at your door wondering if i'll
find the right words to say, but a heart never
lies when it knows what it wants. and if you
invite me in, i promise that i will keep find-
ing you, when the moment is right and even
when it is not because i don't believe that all
good things come to an end.

this is only the beginning
and i can already tell that we
have so much more to see.

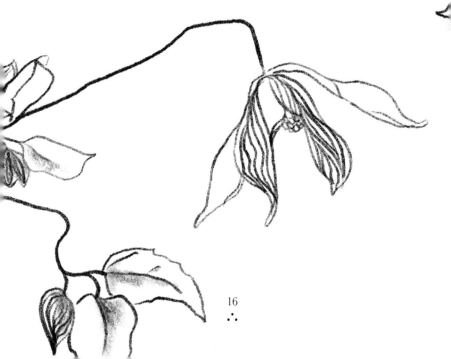

i will never be finished loving you

in this lifetime,
or in any lifetime.

the tide
blushed.

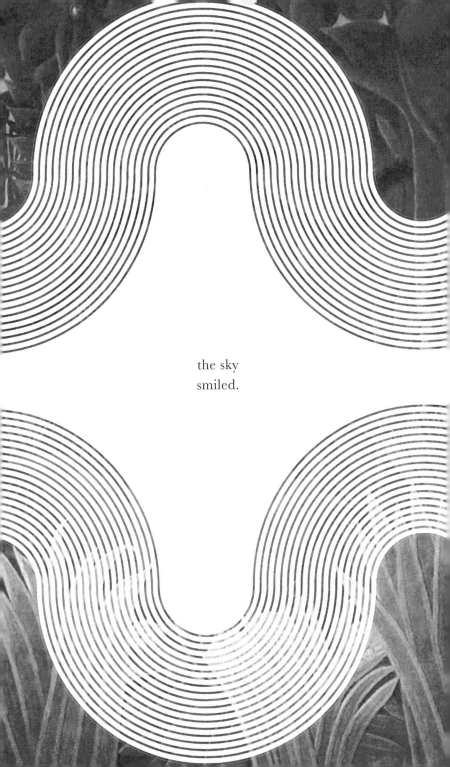

the sky
smiled.

i've always believed that happily ever after
means that you will be here to hold my hand.
that home is you and me watching all four sea-
sons come and go through the kitchen window
and goodbye is just a word we use in the morn-
ing after coffee knowing, "how was your day?"
is never too far behind.

we eat chinese food in bed for dinner and you
keep showing me how to hold the chopsticks
right, even though i've never been able to fig-
ure it out before. you have always been patient
with me and i wish i could say the same about
myself, but you're probably still trying to fig-
ure out what to watch on netflix, and when
you finally do, i'll be half asleep wondering
what i missed.

then you kiss me on the forehead and remind
me to have sweet dreams, and with sleepy eyes
i tell you, "i love you most." because you and
i both know that i like to have the final word.

and the best part is knowing that tomorrow we
will wake up and do it all over again.

and when i open my eyes in the morning,
i already know that you are my favorite part.

this is a reminder
to show yourself more love.

if today feels heavy,
put it down next to forgiveness,
because sometimes the most
vulnerable things need company, too.

i promise that you are more
than your worst days.
and even if they break you,
it is true that time heals all wounds
and eventually yours won't hurt the same.

things that take time:

healing
growing
becoming

there is a special kind of magic that follows
you everywhere you go. and when you
wonder how much more you have left to give,
don't hold on too tightly to what others
think about you.

magic can only be felt by those
who believe in it.

i don't know much,
but i can already tell that someday
i will believe in myself
so much more than you do.

winter slipped away
and *spring* felt like a fast moving train,
but the *summer* days are longer now,
which i've always been particularly fond of,
because a day can never have too much light
or ice cream dates.

every love story is different
and i'm so happy that this is where
ours begins, because you should know
that i love in slow motion and
from where i'm standing i can
tell that you're already starting to *fall*
and i am not too far behind.

i just want you to know
that what i felt was real
and i'm praying for a sign
that it was for you, too.

i promise that the darkness
doesn't last forever.
even when you close your eyes,
the light can still get in.

i outgrew the box you wanted
to keep me in
and it's a miracle that i've already
forgotten who i became
when i was with you.

if you look hard enough,
you will find something inside of you
that believes you can make it through
the bad days.

it doesn't always come naturally,
but when you practice anything over and over
again, eventually it stays.

and if the dream
starts to come undone,
there is another story
waiting to be written.

you will always find who you are
during the hardest times of your life.

∴

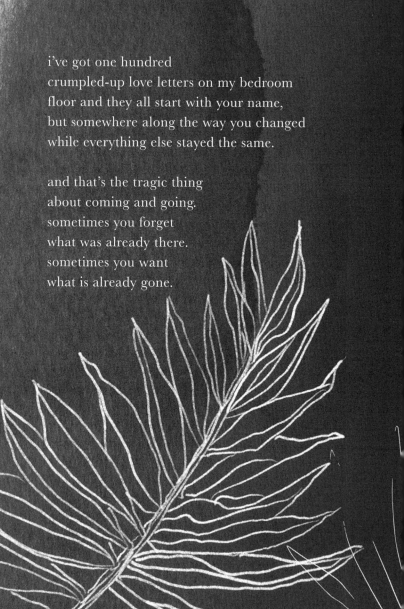

i've got one hundred
crumpled-up love letters on my bedroom
floor and they all start with your name,
but somewhere along the way you changed
while everything else stayed the same.

and that's the tragic thing
about coming and going.
sometimes you forget
what was already there.
sometimes you want
what is already gone.

there is something beautiful
about new beginnings,
the way they fit perfectly in your hands,
like they were made to live there forever.
but as you look down and
wrap your fingers around change,
always remember that there is no failure
in letting go if it starts to hurt.

sometimes saying goodbye
brings us closer to happiness, too.

you could have put a ring from
the quarter machine on my finger
and i still would have said yes one thousand
times, but you never asked the question.

so i held my own hand and
gave myself forever
because at least i was someone
i could depend on.

forever doesn't mean a thing
when you are waiting for a reason
to look forward to tomorrow.

i saw the way you
looked at me
and realized
maybe this is what
it feels like
to be found.

a story like ours was meant for the big screen.
a sunday matinée. two tickets for the sold out
show with popcorn and candy that we snuck
in from the corner store. it's the only time
i break the rules, but you make me want to
break a few more.

our love was so loud that everyone heard it and
when you got down on one knee it brought
them to their feet, and i took your name in an
instant because i knew it was made for me.

everyone wonders what will happen next.
maybe we could write the ending, but not
knowing is my favorite part. and when it gets
to the credits, you squeeze my hand then look
at me and i can already tell that forever will
never be long enough.

my eyes are
looking in the distance
and i can see the
colours changing
with the time of day,
but goodbye doesn't
feel so hard when the light
still remembers my name
no matter how many times
it fades away

i see surrender on the horizon,
and as the sun says goodbye
in shades of rose,
i look up and remember
that leaving can be beautiful
and coming back can be, too.

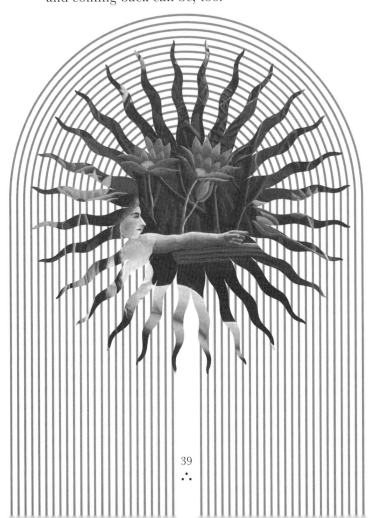

SOUL

why do you love the sun?

it always touches me back.

i left the window open again
and i can hear a storm in the distance.

the ache in my bones is
starting to set in,
but i will hold these open skies
just a little while longer and let go
when the wild tells me it's ready
for change.

i wake up knowing that
you are what you seek
and if you wait long enough,
the sun will turn you to gold.

today, the light found me
and i won't let go.

hope makes mountains worth climbing
and i've never met a sunrise
that didn't move me.

and that's the thing,
you don't even realize how you light up every
room you meet. it's in the way you smile with
your eyes and make a lonely day feel like a
dream come true.

there is a flood inside of me,

but i'm still breathing.

when i was young i wore my shoes 2 sizes
too big because i wanted to give myself room
to grow. my mom left band-aids on the
windowsill (for the blisters and growing pains)
next to a note that said,

nothing can heal without hurting first.

i've carried these words in my pocket for
years next to stories i've been saving for a
rainy day.

and when the storm falls through my hands,
i can see the flowers grow around my feet.
and when they reach in my direction
i realize, this is what it means to be
wild and free.

this is what healing feels like.

i'm still the girl who is stuck in love with you, but i know that the new me will be here any day now, and when she arrives, i hope saying goodbye will be just as easy for me as it was for you.

sometimes you come back to me in my dreams
and it's like you never left my side,
but there's something about being alone
that reminds you how far you can go
without looking back.

i stopped checking my phone for your name
weeks ago and when i think about us i will
remember that i don't need what has left me.
and if i can't sleep tonight, at least i know that
i won't see you while i'm dreaming.

you set my soul on fire

and i kept us warm

it's no secret that
i'm afraid of change,
but spring and fall showed me
that growing and falling
is something we can all do
day after day
and everyone will still call it
beautiful.

when you feel like you are
losing yourself,
hold on tight to hope
and let the pieces go
like autumn leaves
on a small town street
where everyone knows your name
and nobody forgets a masterpiece
that looks like you.

trust the process

you call me a backseat driver,
but you and i both know that
i'll never leave your side.
these winding roads are endless
and knowing that some of the
greatest stories have yet to be written
is proof that our adventure
is just getting started.

when you close your eyes,
please don't forget about me,
because even when it's dark
i am still reaching out for you
and i'm just waiting for you to
see me.

you made it so easy to love you. you made it so easy to love you.
you made it so easy to love you. you made it so easy to love you.
you made it so easy to love you. you made it so easy to love you.
you made it so easy to love you. you made it so easy to love you.
you made it so easy to love you. you made it so easy to love you.
you made it so easy to love you. you made it so easy to love you.
you made it so easy to love you. you made it so easy to love you.
you made it so easy to love you. you made it so easy to love you.
you made it so easy to love you. you made it so easy to love you.
but harder to love me. but harder to love me. but harder to love me.
you made it so easy to love you. you made it so easy to love you.
you made it so easy to love you. you made it so easy to love you.
you made it so easy to love you. you made it so easy to love you.
you made it so easy to love you. you made it so easy to love you.
you made it so easy to love you. you made it so easy to love you.
you made it so easy to love you. you made it so easy to love you.
you made it so easy to love you. you made it so easy to love you.
you made it so easy to love you. you made it so easy to love you.
you made it so easy to love you. you made it so easy to love you.
you made it so easy to love you. you made it so easy to love you.
you made it so easy to love you. you made it so easy to love you.
you made it so easy to love you. you made it so easy to love you.
you made it so easy to love you. you made it so easy to love you.
you made it so easy to love you. you made it so easy to love you.

if you forgive the worst,
then it will forgive you, too.

it seems like it's been a lifetime,
but i still feel the same.
maybe it's a slow burn
waiting for me to find the bright side,
but you can't see the sun
if you don't look outside.

they say what doesn't kill you makes you
stronger and i want to be remembered for
something greater than this.

sometimes change is uncomfortable
because you find yourself
walking down a road that you've never
been on before.
the street lights are flickering,
but even when they go out,
you aren't scared of the things you cannot
see, and you can't help but feel
like this looks a lot like the future
you've been waiting for.

maybe it was a waste of time
or maybe it was everything you ever needed.

i was that "dream big" kid who saw
the whole world in one afternoon.
i drew pictures that were larger than life
and folded paper cranes with hands
that set them free whenever they were ready.
i still wonder all the places they have gone,
but i'm pretty sure i'll see them again soon,
because they flew south for winter and spring
is right around the corner.

my bedroom was one part jungle and
one part african safari, depending on the
time of day. the lions spoke a language only
i could understand and even still, i can hear
them call my name.

everything was perfectly imperfect in the
most beautiful way,
and i hope i never forget what it feels like
to be both at the same time.

why do we grow up
and stop believing
that anything is possible
when life takes the time to show us
that everything is.

you said i love you
like it was poetry,
and i held on to it
like it was true.

everything felt right
when you were standing next to me,
but when you left i still felt the same.
and then i realized that i was the one
who carried the light
and you were just a temporary fix.

never stop making
your own light.

they say patience is a virtue,
but they never tell you how long
a heart should keep waiting
for when the moment is right.
maybe i just have a fear of missing out,
but the sad truth is that
you loved me too late
and i showed up on time.

i picked up all the broken pieces
and turned them into something beautiful.

there was a map next to my heart
that led me straight to you,

it was a no traffic on the interstate
kind of love.
a shout it from the rooftops
kind of love.
a billboard in the middle of times square
kind of love.

i fell for you in an instant.
you fell for me all at once.

and for the first time in my life
i met someone who wanted to
meet me halfway.

tell your story
even if you think no one is listening.
live your life like you might
be gone tomorrow.
be so unapologetically you that
they can't help but wonder
how they've lived so long
without doing the same.
run free like the wild
has something to lose.
stop to catch your breath
because the perfect storm
is still trying to catch up.

and don't you see?
no one else is the hero here,
because it has always been you.

sometimes i am both the bandage and the
wound. kissing my mistakes to make them
feel better, praying they will heal so i can
forget they were ever there.

today, my bedroom is a confessional.
i found healing and forgiveness hiding
underneath the bed where i buried the
things that no longer serve me.

i think this is what hope feels like.
the weight has lifted off my shoulders
and the scars don't look the same.

i love you doesn't mean the same thing
when it's said a moment too late.

so i buried the hatchet and left with all the
grace that i could carry in my arms.
and what a beautiful thing it is,
being able to reach for the sky
now that my hands are free.

i could have let you haunt me,
but instead i made friends with
the ghost of you and it feels so good
to fly again.

when you wonder where i'm going,
i promise, i'll be back before you miss me.

at the end of the day,
all i want is to spend
every sunset with you.

SANCTUARY

nothing in the wild ever stays the same.
even now i can feel the colour
of my heart changing.

there was something special about those
summer nights. when the sun stayed up past
my bedtime and the ice cream truck was the
only alarm clock that could get me out of bed.
my favorite part was when it came back again
for lunch and dinner. i was a sucker for snow cones
and push-up pops. what my parents didn't
realize is that they were suckers, too. i was
equal parts sticky and sweet for three months
straight, but i didn't mind. the sprinklers were
on 24/7 and a storm was never too far away.

we liked to ride our bikes in the rain and
pretend that we were from the other side of the
world. we spoke a language that only we could
understand—i think all best friends do. when
sunset came we were on a mission. you carried
the net (wide enough to catch our dreams) and i
held the jar (full of magic). there was no field too
big for our eyes. i think we touched every
firefly that summer, and when we set them free,
i always knew that a part of us went with them.

and i still wonder how much we have left to see.

when the jungle takes over inside of you,
you can either cut it down or let it grow.

there is a broken compass in my pocket and i've
been flying for days, but i have never been very
good at following directions. they think i am a
lost cause, but i promise i'm just lost *(in every
way i am meant to be)* and even if i forget my way
back home i know there is a story inside of me
waiting to be read again.

even in the summer
we held each other
like it was cold outside.

if i'm sure of anything at all
it's that i will never get tired
of growing old with you.

your voice
is soft like morning.
and when you ask me what i mean
i will walk with you to tomorrow
because every beginning starts
with your name.

and this,
this is what forever feels like.
you built a home around us
and the walls tell stories
that we never want to forget.

and when you said i was the colour of your favorite dream, i knew you could see what i was made of.

sometimes spring can
feel so heavy after all that rain,
but when you open your eyes to change,
you can't help but see all of the possibilities
that come with starting over again.

they say that i should learn from my
mistakes, but what they don't see is that this
is what trying looks like. this is me getting out
of bed when the pillows asked me to stay all
day and it took everything in me not to listen.

healing looks different on everyone and it's
not easy putting one foot in front of the other
when someone is holding you back because
the way you're moving forward doesn't look
the way they think it should.

YOU'RE

SO

DEN

i thought we were a once in a lifetime
kind of thing because when you opened the
door for me that first night, i felt like i was
walking into a dream come true, but you
became my worst nightmare.

i should have known that it was over
when i told you my secret
and i became yours.
so i left before the after-party—
nothing good happens there anyway
and i don't have it in me
to make another mistake,
saying things i don't mean to
people who will forget me
tomorrow.

instead, i'm sitting on my front porch
waiting for the sun to come up,
because all i need is a little bit of
light to remind me that i am
so much more than the person
you tried to hide.

it's never been so easy
to get up after falling.

i dream in colour
in a world where
everything feels so black and white.
and if i know anything about myself,
it's that i'm too untamed for
a monochromatic life.

no one can live with
their eyes closed forever,
so i think i'll paint the town
in every shade of spring.
because the truth is, the wild
has always been our neutral ground.
we just need to remember
that the past is behind us like
last winter's snow, and
there's so much more to life
than trying to prove
who is right or wrong
when the sky reminds us
that all of our shadows
look the same
no matter the time
of day.

i wear summer on my skin
like your favorite oversized vintage tee
that you forgot in my closet.

there is still so much room for both of us
here.

and i still wonder if you left it behind
on purpose so you had something to come
back for.

when i couldn't see in the dark,
i called out your name and
you became my sun
in the middle of a cloudy day.

we put it all on the line.
date night at the coffee table,
scrabble pieces spread out
in front of us with an empty pizza box
on the floor.

you are a walking dictionary
so i don't think the odds are in my favor,
but to be honest, there aren't enough letters
in the alphabet for me to spell
how much i love you, anyway.

we were just two people
blinded by the word *forever,*
writing a story that had no end in sight,
with nothing to lose
and everything to win.

5 things you might need to read today:

1. it's okay if getting up is the
hardest thing you'll do today.

2. you don't have to smile when it
hurts.

3. the sun never stops shining,
even when the darkness comes
to hide its light.

4. goodbye isn't always forever,
but even if it is, something new
will find you when you're not looking.

5. there are so many different versions
of yourself that you're going to meet.
welcome each with open arms and
don't be afraid to say goodbye when
you are ready.

don't spend your life waiting for the weekend
or for that summer vacation 7 months away.
and if you're looking for love to come knock-
ing at your door on a friday night, i promise
it will find you when it's ready. dinner is over-
rated anyway, when a picnic in the park is so
much more poetic.

if you stop wishing the time away, life will not
be able to pass by without your permission.
because one day you will look back and won-
der where it all went and the pictures will be a
nice reminder of what you would have missed,
but living in the moment is so much better
when you're sitting in the front row seat.

it felt hopeful
like a *maybe*,
but it was over
like a season finale.

i held on for too long
and you overstayed your welcome,
but the worst part is
that it only took a second
for you to break my heart
and forever for me to
forgive you.

for what it's worth, it was a silent pain.
the kind where the sunset fades from the sky
slowly and then all at once. and we both look
up, knowing that it was beautiful while it
lasted.

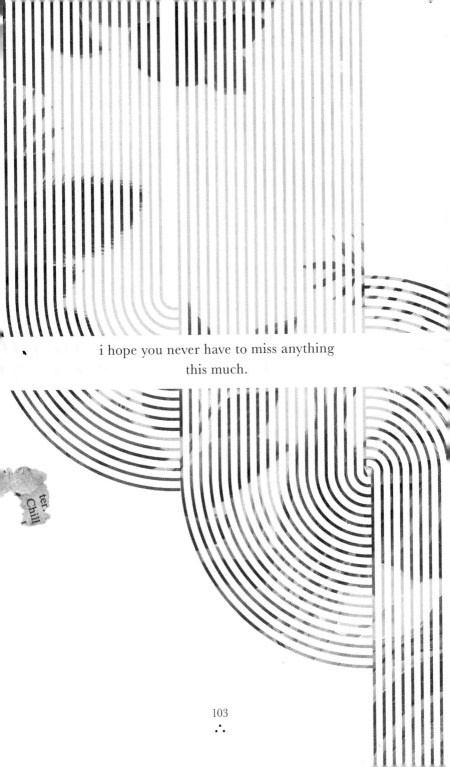

i hope you never have to miss anything
this much.

∴

it said *no turn on red,* but i've never been good at reading the signs or spotting the flags waving in front of me. that's the thing about seeing the best in people, you believe that everything will get better if you wait just a little bit longer. maybe it was all in my head. maybe you just needed to see it, too.

somewhere along the way i learned to listen to my intuition. sometimes, life is like watching a movie you've already seen before and hoping that the ending will change. sometimes, it's knowing what happens before it even gets to the end.

when i turn around,
all i see is the memory of you
and a past i want to forget.
but when i stopped looking back,
i found myself and learned
how to smile again.

i hope that you did, too.

MAYBE IT'S

LUCK.

MAYBE IT'S

SERENDIPITY.

when you learn how to love yourself,
there is something inside of you
that starts to change.
they say nothing can grow
without the light,
but they haven't seen
the garden growing inside of me
that started with a lot of
darkness and a little bit of hope.

the light can't help anything
if the seed isn't planted first.

they call me too emotional,
but no one can grow if they don't let go.

it's okay to cry

you were everything
i never knew i needed
until you said my name
and gave me a reason to listen.

and even if you feel like you're losing me,
just know that i will keep finding you
if you let me.

i learned to colour my sky with courage
because wide open spaces used to make me
feel like i was already ~~failing~~ falling before
i even had a chance to get my feet off the
ground. but when you take the time to watch
the sun rise after it's been hiding behind the
night, it makes you believe you can do
anything.

no matter where you have been,
there is a light at the end of the
tunnel waiting for you.
and as your eyes begin to adjust
to the brighter side,
always remember you're here
because you walked yourself
home, and it's okay if you're still
trying to find who you are
meant to be.

you can never meet the best day of your life
if you don't get to know some of your worst.

you are like a piece of art hanging on the
walls of a city museum.

people can't help but stop to admire you.
they stand in silence, trying to understand
what makes you, you. they call you priceless
for a reason and when they leave, it's no
wonder they can't get you off of their mind.

no one ever forgets the things that move
them.

i believed we were going to last forever
like the matching tattoos we got on a whim.
we lived in a small house in a college town
and lived off of saturday football games and
indian food. it was a simple kind of love, but
it was all i ever needed. that's the thing about
falling in love in your early twenties; you
believe anything your heart touches is
invincible.

and now the only things we have in common
are a past we both moved on from and ink
buried underneath our skin. sometimes i
wonder where it all went wrong, but what i
know for sure is that it's okay that it did.

i picked up right where you left me
and said goodbye to your name and
all of the photographs hanging on our walls
because you can't keep loving yourself when
you try to hold on to someone who wants to
leave.

goodbye was so permanent.
forgetting you was, too.

maybe you are lost,
or maybe this is you
waiting to be found
by someone like me.

i am lost.
i am home.

ORACLE

i met you on your birthday in the pouring
rain at the small town dive bar down the
street, and when you smiled at me, the rest
was history.

we took the long way home with the convert-
ible top down because thirty looked so good
on you and summer gives everyone a reason
to let go.

there was no room for mistakes on that
friday night when everything was so meant to
be. it was the beginning of a love story and
here we are, still writing it in our hearts. and
in the stars.

SPARKS

FLY

i look up at the sky
and my arms are still catching up
to the rest of me.
it's so high up here,
this bird's-eye view.
where anything seems possible
because everything is within reach.

that's the thing about hope;
just because you can't see it,
that doesn't mean it's not there.

INVISIBLE

F R I E N D

they say to stay close
to the people who feel like
sunlight and my only hope
is that i can be the light in your sky
just like you are in mine.

i was looking for a place to call mine,
so you grabbed my hand and promised me
every tomorrow that waited for us.
that's what i love about you and me.
forever isn't a maybe
and home is never too far away.

HOME

IS WHERE THE HEART IS

i'm still trying to find where i dropped my
heart because i don't see it on my sleeve
where it usually is. i'm the kind of person
who leaves my love out in the open for
everyone to see, but i'm learning that i need
to keep it safe from people who like to steal
the show.

if you find it before i do, please handle it with
care because i'm running out of glue and i'm
tired of trying to put myself back together.

october faded away
and the days are shorter now,
but there's something about
january that gives everyone
a reason to be hopeful.

a fresh start.
a new beginning.

something to look forward to when
everything feels so grey.

WINTER

MIGRATION

the things that are
meant to come back
always will.

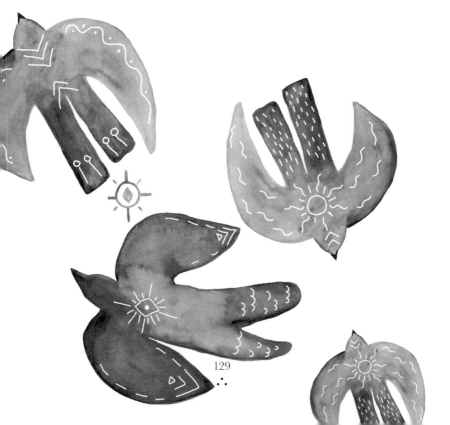

129
∴

you read my mind
like i was your favorite book
and i didn't want you
to put me down
because there was still
so much for me to show you,
but the beautiful part
was that you already knew
what was going to happen next
and i did, too.

KINDRED

SPIRIT

you should know that it's okay to feel out
of place. i think being in the right place at
the right time is overrated anyway, because
taking a wrong turn has the potential to be so
much more exciting.

nothing wild and free is ever planned.

sometimes it is messy.
sometimes it is unexpected.

and that's what makes it real.
that's what makes it worth it.

i promise to keep finding you even when you are lost. i will hold you up if you fall and be the light when you can't see. i'll be the hand that leads you to safer ground and i'll carry you through every season if it means i get to be by your side through it all.

I'LL SEE YOU

ON THE OTHER SIDE

sometimes all it takes is believing
that you deserve better.

don't stand in the dark
when the sun is just around the corner
waiting to help you grow.

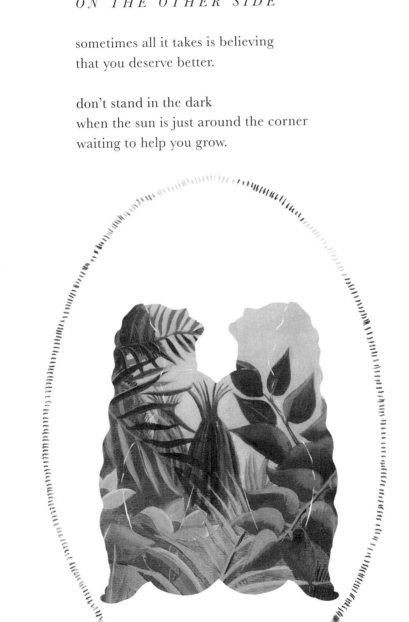

i'll never forget the night we met,
your eyes were full of stars
and they were looking at me.

i fell for you faster than my favorite song
and i know you still can't get me
out of your head.

7 MINUTES

IN HEAVEN

i'm not one to pray out loud,
but i always find myself looking up
for answers. and what i know for sure
is that i want to be wherever you are,
so if there's a heaven, i know that's
where you'll be, so i will do whatever
it takes to get there, too.

one day i will look back and be grateful that my own love was enough during times like this. i will carry grace in my hands and look in the mirror every day and admire the person looking back at me. my voice will learn not to shake, but for those times when it does, i will remember that the storm doesn't last forever and that there's still a reason to love the rain.

DANCING

IN THE RAIN

i hope you will see that it's okay to be
both the thunder and lightning.
never forget what you're fighting for,
because i've never met a storm that
didn't make me look up and wonder
what might happen next.

sometimes the clouds part and the rain
fades away into the distance and other times
it stays awhile and makes you want to stand
outside and let go, too.

you call me a poet,
but sometimes i hold the pen in my hand
and the words do not find me.
how do you write love on a page when
there is nothing that sounds as beautiful
as you?

i don't know if i'll ever be able to fill
this blank space, but i promise, i will never
stop trying.

I WANT YOU

TO LOVE ME

never forget to love yourself first.
be everything you need on your best days,
but especially on your worst because
you deserve to see the bright side of
everything and i know that if you look
hard enough, you will find it.

be brave in a world that tries
to scare you into submission and use
your voice to speak your mind—
it is a beautiful place that has
the power to change the way anyone
looks at the sky.

and if somewhere along the way you start to
lose sight of who you are, don't leave yourself
behind. just follow your own lead and
you will find that you are exactly
where you are meant to be.

i have never needed anyone
to be the hero of my story,
but i'm the kind of person who keeps
the things i love close to my chest,
because there's a chance
that anything my heart touches
will stay forever.

i guess that's the optimist in me—
finding something to believe in
and hoping that it wants to stay.

POCKET

CHANGE

time brings the truth to the surface
and no matter how hard we try to rewrite
the end of our story, it will always be the
same.

i won't keep breaking my own heart
to make yours feel better.

and you shouldn't either.

you were so unexpected.
you were my favorite plot twist.

TWIST

OF FATE

you said you were a lost soul
and in that moment i knew
you were going to be my greatest
adventure.

we held hands on these streets
knowing that this was our home
away from home.

the place that calls our name and we will
always come running back because
this city made us realize that forever
is on our side and that magic is real
if you are willing to believe that it's been
there all along.

NEW ORLEANS

PARADE

our love was loud and fearless
like a marching band
in the middle of mardi gras.

their eyes were on us
and i couldn't take mine
off yours.

i knew you by heart
and you knew me like
the back of your hand.

it was the beginning of something special
before i even knew your name.

TWIN

FLAME

i left before the credits
because it was an ending i didn't need to see.
and i don't need your late night apologies
because i stopped setting myself on fire
to keep you warm.

it's funny how the dark doesn't scare you
anymore when you're the one holding the
light.

i hope you never forget
what it felt like to believe
tomorrow was on our side.
i hope you will remember me
in the best light, because the
way i shined was also a
reflection of you.

goodbye doesn't have to be
a shouting match in our living room
when it can be a standing ovation.
we tried our best and that's all
anyone could hope for.

and as i stand here with tears
falling from my eyes,
just know that it's because it was a
feel good story and it's okay to be
happy and sad at the same time.

WILL YOU REMEMBER ME

TOMORROW

you are the person
who looks at me and gives
me so many reasons
to look forward to
what will happen next.

i see you while i'm sleeping
and the best part
is knowing you'll still be here
when i open my eyes
in the morning.

A DREAM

COME TRUE

i pinch myself every once in a while
to make sure that this is real.
and then i remember
that nothing is impossible
when you believe that good things
deserve to happen to you.

you are my laugh in the middle of a bad day.
my kiss on the forehead when you think i'm
asleep. my calm before the storm. my smile
when it hurts. my shoulder to cry on. my
person. my love. my everything.

HE LOVES ME

HE LOVES ME NOT

there are a thousand little pieces of me
scattered on the floor and they each tell a
story about you and me. we had a love meant
for the record books, but you can't always be
the best when the worst finally catches up to
you.

no one tells you how to prepare your heart
for breaking, but what i know for sure is that
i can choose how to put myself back together
and even if it hurts, at least i will know that
all of the pain meant something because it
was real.

anything that makes
your heart smile is worth
reaching for no matter
how far away it seems.

J O Y

RIDE

let's take the long way home, drive down the
country road and chase the sunset until we
are with the stars. let's dance in the middle
of the highway under the only street light in
town. i'll sing your favorite song if you
promise to lead the way.

and i'll walk with you 'til sunrise because i
don't want to close my eyes just yet. this is
one of those stories i want to last forever and
if i read it slow enough, maybe it will.

sometimes i say *i love you* in the middle of the
night. your eyes are closed and you are
sleeping, but i know that you can hear me.
sometimes you whisper it back to me
and i laugh, knowing you have no idea what is
going on, but that's not to say that you mean it
any less. it's endearing, really.

i think that love is a lot like muscle memory.

a heart never forgets.
a heart never stops.

and there's a voice that knows
all the words by heart.

THE ONE

FOR ME

there isn't a mountain my eyes can't climb
and even though the stars are high,
my dreams are always higher.

sometimes i reach for them,
but sometimes they reach for me.

how lucky am i to be the first thing you touch
after every hello and the last before every
goodbye.

CHASING

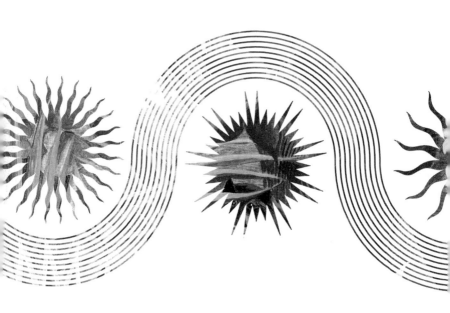

SUNSETS

even though i've never been very good
at keeping up, there is something
beautiful about trying to catch something
before it leaves.

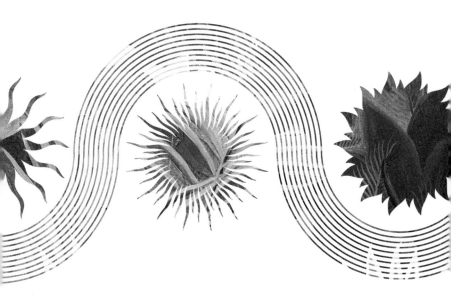

it's hard to leave when you're in the middle
of a good dream.

to be continued . . .

WITH GRATITUDE

to jarett, my person. thank you for always
shining a light on the things that matter.

to mom, dad, larry and family, without your
love i could have never grown into the person
i am.

to jess, my soul sister. my sun in the middle of
a cloudy day.

to sam, my kindred spirit. thank you for
always being so close.

to james and courtney, thank you for helping
me keep all of my dreams alive.

to kaya. the sweetest wild child i have ever
met. i wrote so many of these words in your
company and i smile knowing that pieces of
you are scattered in these pages.

to the andrews mcmeel family, thank you for
giving my dreams a place to land.

to you, thank you for finding these words
and giving them a home. knowing they have
touched you and you have touched them is
the greatest gift my heart could ever know.

All of the jungle paintings found throughout this book are from my favorite painter, Henri Rousseau. His art makes all of my dark days brighter and I hope that it can do the same for you.

Andrews McMeel Publishing
a division of Andrews McMeel Universal
1130 Walnut Street, Kansas City, Missouri 64106

www.andrewsmcmeel.com

22 23 24 25 26 RR2 10 9 8 7 6 5 4 3 2 1

ISBN: 978-1-5248-7579-4

Library of Congress Control Number:
2022938600

Editor: Patty Rice
Designer: wilder
Production Editor: David Shaw
Production Manager: Shona Burns

ATTENTION: SCHOOLS AND BUSINESSES
Andrews McMeel books are available at quantity
discounts with bulk purchase for educational,
business, or sales promotional use. For information,
please e-mail the Andrews McMeel Publishing
Special Sales Department:
specialsales@amuniversal.com

wilderpoetry.com

follow the visual story on instagram:
wilderpoetry